AUTOS ACROSS AMERICA

AUTOS

ACROSS AMERICA

A Bibliography of
Transcontinental Automobile
Travel : 1903—1940

By CAREY S. BLISS

Los Angeles DAWSON'S BOOK SHOP 1972

DEDICATED TO MY FATHER

LESLIE E. BLISS

An auto pioneer himself, who drove me
on my first transcontinental trip

PREFACE

The germ of this bibliography was nurtured almost twenty years ago when I purchased for a very modest sum two automobile juveniles, Clarence Young's The Motor Boys Overland, *New York,* c.1906, *and Katherine Stokes'* The Motor Maids Across the Continent, *New York,* c.1911. *The central theme of both books is a transcontinental auto trip across the United States. This theme intrigued me as to its source and I began to wonder if printed accounts of actual auto trips across the continent did exist. If the overland covered wagon pioneers wrote down their experiences, perhaps the transcontinental auto pioneers did the same thing? A search through the volumes of the* Readers' Guide to Periodical Literature *between 1895 and 1910 turned up a few early periodical accounts. Magazines such as* Sunset *and* Overland Monthly *between 1900 and 1910 were filled with automobile articles on touring in the west and occasionally statements, predictions, and speculations about transcontinental auto routes. Even the national magazines had automobile numbers with articles on long distance auto travel as, for example,* Scribner's Magazine *for February, 1914 with an article by Henry B. Joy,"Transcontinental Trails.–Their development and what they mean to this country," and a series of eight photographs by Earle Harrison, reproduced in color, entitled "Scenes on old trails. The transcontinental motor-roads of to-morrow."*

The location of separately printed book and pamphlet accounts was a more difficult chase. Previously published bibliographies were of little or no use. Mary Tucker's bibliography, Books of the Southwest; a general bibliography, *yielded a few leads but many of the titles, when carefully examined, did not prove to be complete transcontinental trips. A search of the automobile subject columns of the early volumes of the* United States Catalog *turned up a few more prospects, enough so that a want list was drawn up and sent to a few booksellers. However, the most productive source proved to be the personal examination of the automobile and travel sections of the rare and second hand book stores, followed by the careful reading of catalogues from other book dealers. As the collection progressed and my wants became known, many dealers would quote titles on their shelves. A number of scarce and unknown pamphlets thus came my way. It might be appropriate here to publicly acknowledge the help of the following booksellers who went out of their way to locate and quote certain titles to me: the late Charles Yale and his partner, Philip S. Brown, of Pasadena; Glen Dawson of Dawson's Book Shop, Los Angeles; Maxwell Hunley of Beverly Hills; and Lester Roberts of San Francisco. Many other booksellers across this country contributed knowingly or unknowingly to this work. To those mentioned and to those not mentioned, my grateful thanks.*

It was not until the gathering of these titles had progressed for some time, and the collection had reached a respectable size, that the idea of producing a bibliography came about. Actually, it must be confessed that it was Glen Dawson who proposed it. He suggested doing a descriptive bibliography in detail. The starting date would be the first recorded transcontinental auto account and the finishing date would be the point when the trips became so commonplace that they were no longer recorded in book or pamphlet form.

When the decision to proceed with a formal bibliography was made all the previous search programs were continued and intensified. Later, a photo copy of all the catalog cards in the automobiling section of the *Automotive History Collection* at the Detroit Public Library was obtained. It was gratifying to find that of the 119 titles listed, only four were new additions to the bibliography. This information coupled with the fact that only one new title had turned up in a year's time from all other sources, brought about the decision to close the books, put the bibliography in final shape, and submit it for publication. No doubt as soon as the first proof sheets are received a number of titles will turn up. But after all, isn't that what bibliographies are for?

All items listed are in my own collection or that of the Huntington Library, unless otherwise noted.

Mention was made earlier of the valuable assistance rendered by the booksellers, near and far. But special thanks must go to my wife, Amelia, for her unswerving support in so many ways—for her typing of the manuscript, her correction of numerous errors, her standardization of entries and smoothing of the text, her monetary support of the project (paying the book bills), and, last but not least, her patience and enthusiasm from beginning to end. Without her help, the project would not have gotten off the ground.

C. S. B.

San Gabriel, California
October 1971

LIST OF CONTENTS

PREFACE *p. vii*

INTRODUCTION *xiii*

BIBLIOGRAPHY I

REJECTED TITLES 54

INDEX 57

ILLUSTRATIONS

Across the Continent in a Winton at page	*xiii*
From Ocean to Ocean in a Winton	4
Three Times Across the Continent on Weed Chain Tire Grips	5
5000 Miles Overland	12
From New York to Los Angeles	13
Across the Continent by the Lincoln Highway	16
It Might Have Been Worse	17
How's the Road?	32
Across the Continent Twice in Three Weeks	33
America: First, Fast & Furious	48
Double-Crossing America by Motor	49

See item 1, *page* 1

INTRODUCTION

The modern motorist who takes for granted well-maintained highways, free and accurate maps, service stations every few miles, and ample accommodations for food and lodging may well wonder why the hazards and hardships of early transcontinental travel were undertaken. What motivated these automobile pioneers? It was certainly not the same desires that drew the covered wagon pioneers across the plains and through the mountains. Gold and good free land were gone by the time these auto pioneers began their treks. The earliest accounts indicate that the spirit of adventure and a desire to be first were strong factors. Several abortive attempts were made before the first successful coast to coast trip was made in 1903. Perhaps the earliest was that made by Mr. and Mrs. John D. Davis who left New York City on July 13, 1899, destination San Francisco. On August 19 their fragile two-seater, make unknown, arrived in Detroit, Michigan after 25 breakdowns. Nothing more was ever heard of the expedition and so it must be assumed that the trip ended in Detroit or possibly a few miles further on. Many of the early trips were made by professional drivers to advertise the worthiness of a certain car or various automotive accessories. Through all the accounts, however, even those printed as late as the 1920s and '30s, runs a sense of pride and achievement, almost a trace of the pioneer feeling of independence – a feeling of independence which they did not get in travelling across the country by train where their lives and fortunes were in the hands of the train crew and not themselves. The desire to get away from the congestion of an increasingly urbanized society and to explore the vast reaches of the United States is also frequently mentioned as an inducement for undertaking the journey.

In the following bibliography I have attempted to record all the printed accounts of transcontinental automobile travel across the United States from 1903 to 1940. 1903 was the year of the first successful crossing. An arbitrary cut-off date was set up at 1940 although no account later than 1938 has been included. It was felt that by that date the excitement and adventures of a transcontinental auto trip were gone. It had, indeed, become an every day occurrence. The few accounts published after 1940 concerned themselves with the panorama of American life and scenery and not to the hazards and mechanics of the trip.

I have patterned the work in general following the plan set up by Henry R. Wagner in his *The Plains and the Rockies, a bibliography of original narratives of travel and adventure*, 1800–1865, with a brief bibliographical description, an account of the trip, and some personal impressions and comments about the work. The listing is arranged chronologically by the date of the trip and not by publication date which sometimes occurred much later.

A few criteria have been arbitrarily set up for inclusion in this list which it might be well to mention here. The vehicles must be four wheeled and powered by gasoline, steam, or electricity. I do not believe any of the cars mentioned in the present listing were powered by steam or electricity, but they should not be excluded. The trip must include the more difficult roads and mountain passes of the western states. A trip may start anywhere east of the Mississippi but must end up on the west coast. West to east trips must begin on the west coast and cross the Mississippi River. As a matter of fact, all or nearly all west to east trips recorded do wind up on the Atlantic coast. Even before 1903 long auto trips all through the states east of the Mississippi were common and several accounts were published.

In a column entitled "Books that should be written" in *Publishers' Weekly*, October 6, 1920, p. 1129, is the terse statement: "Motor trips anywhere in the U. S. Also transcontinental trips. Gladding and Post are popular in spite of mediocre quality." The columnist was referring to Effie Price Gladding, *Across the Continent by the Lincoln Highway*, New York, 1915 and Emily Post, *By Motor to the Golden Gate*, New York and London, 1916 (both titles are recorded in the following bibliography). As professional guides, these books left much to be desired as this columnist indicated, but there were local route books available for the motorist as early as 1909. The Automobile Club of Southern California issued its first tour book of the California area early in 1909. Transcontinental road guides were available as early as 1915. The Goodrich Tire Company issued a detailed road guide from New York to Los Angeles via the southern route in that year and the Touring Information Bureau of America issued its *Automobile Route Book* containing photographs, strip maps, and detailed information of all transcontinental routes the same year. From the comments made by some of the users, these very early road guides were sometimes unreliable and of dubious value. These professional route or guide books are not within the provenance of this bibliography though they are numerous and important enough to warrant their own listing some day. I believe the type of book this columnist wanted, however, *is* the provenance of this bibliography. A perusal of the titles listed hereafter may answer that statement.

By 1924, however, the auto tourist had seven separate routes to choose from if he contemplated a transcontinental jaunt. None of them would have been considered freeways or even highways in our present understanding of the terms, but they were dignified by colored markers on posts and telephone poles to reassure the driver that he was on the right road. The seven routes and the colored markers as listed in *The Automobile Road Book with Descriptions of Highways*, Chicago, *c.* 1924, prepared by Rand McNally and Company, are as follows:

1. The Lincoln Highway, New York to San Francisco across the central United States; red, white and blue marker, overprinted "Lincoln L Highway."

2. National Old Trails Road, Washington, D. C. to Los Angeles following in part the Santa Fe Trail; red, white and blue marker, "National Old Trails Road" printed beneath.

3. Theodore Roosevelt International Highway, a northern route from Portland, Maine, to Portland, Oregon; white, red and white marker overprinted T R, "Theodore Roosevelt International Highway" printed beneath.

4. The Yellowstone Trail, Plymouth Rock to Puget Sound via Illinois, north and west through the Canadian border states; yellow square overprinted with "Yellowstone Trail" in circle with an arrow in the center.

5. Bankhead Highway, Washington, D. C. south and west through the southern states to California; yellow, white and yellow marker, overprinted B H with "Bankhead Highway" printed beneath.

6. The Old Spanish Trail, Florida to California; red, white and yellow marker overprinted O S T, "The Old Spanish Trail" printed beneath.

7. Pikes Peak Ocean to Ocean Highway, New York and Philadelphia to San Francisco, following generally the fortieth parallel; red and white marker with "Pikes Peak Ocean to Ocean Highway" printed beneath.

The two principal routes travelled were the Lincoln Highway and the National Old Trails Road. The Lincoln Highway was the first transcontinental route, being proposed in 1912, but not fully completed for general use until about 1919. The National Old Trails Road is now known as Route 66, fabled in story and song. It might be interesting to note here that the first all trans-

Canadian highway from the Atlantic Ocean to the Pacific Ocean was not officially completed until September 3, 1962.

Considering the fact that even today most travellers keep at least a mileage and expense account of their trips and many compile detailed diaries, it is perhaps surprising that more trips were not put into print. Many, of course, may have been published in local newspapers and journals which would have been impossible to locate for this bibliography. Then, too, a number of early transcontinental trips may exist in manuscript, accompanied by original photographs, tucked away in attics or closet shelves, almost forgotten by their compiler. A few might well be worthy of publication some day.

These pioneer auto accounts occupy only a small segment of the vast literature connected with automobiliana. The excellent automotive history collection of the Detroit Public Library is very large but only a small number of titles are concerned with travel and touring and many of those are not transcontinental trips. Two local private collections I have seen or know about have very few books of this type when compared with the large numbers of histories, manuals, guide books and other printed items relating to the automobile. Even so, the dream of crossing the country by auto was mentioned often while the automobile was still in its infancy.

What of the value of these books for the historian or as literature? Even a hasty reading of some of these titles will reveal that they have preserved in writing, often unwittingly, an account of some of the American folkways and mores of the first third of this century. As far as automotive history is concerned, they have captured in print a small but glamorous, often humorous side of this vast industry. Most of the titles recorded here have very little literary value and some are, frankly, very badly written. Well known or even minor writers do not glorify the pages of this bibliography with the possible exception of Katherine Hulme, Emily Post, and the illustrator, James Montgomery Flagg. Two titles which may stand the test of time for their literary value are Dallas Lore Sharp's *The Better Country*, 1928 and Lewis Gannett's *Sweet Land*, 1934, second edition 1937. Both of them are written as a series of short essays and each, in its own way, seems to capture the flavor of America at that particular time.

While gathering and examining titles for this bibliography, I was struck by the number of times a title or superficial examination of a book would lead one into believing it should be included in the list. Therefore, partly as a defence against critics and partly to save others the trouble, I have included at the end of the bibliography a short-title list of rejected books with, usually, a reason for its rejection. This list has been alphabetically arranged by author rather than chronologically as is the bibliography.

Always in compiling a bibliography of this sort there are titles which one is tempted to enter but, because of the limits self-imposed by the bibliographer, they must be excluded. But if they cannot be included, they can at least be mentioned. One of Sinclair Lewis's earliest novels was *Free Air*, New York, 1919, an account of a girl and her father driving across country from Minneapolis to Seattle. The careful detail and descriptions prove beyond doubt that the author experienced such a trip first hand, but because it is written as fiction it has been excluded. Four other titles by well-known writers were not listed because the trips were taken after 1940 or were not primarily concerned with the automobile trip itself.

1. Henry Miller. *Air Conditioned Nightmare*. New York, 1945. Miller comments on America while driving from New York to Los Angeles in 1940.

2. John Steinbeck. *Travels with Charlie*. New York, 1962. Steinbeck's delightful bestseller account of his travels across America in a camper truck accompanied only by his French poodle.

3. Erskine Caldwell. *Around About America*. New York, 1964.

4. William Saroyan. *Short Drive, Sweet Chariot*. New York, 1966. Saroyan's impressions on a trip from New York to Fresno driving a 1914 Lincoln in 1963.

In conclusion, a few observations on collecting these titles are offered here, bearing in mind that these are my own thoughts after searching for them for over the past nineteen years. A number of these titles are fairly easy to acquire. A want list of all the titles sent to five or ten book dealers specializing in Americana might result in quotations offering 15 or 20 of the titles. Most difficult to run down would be the early automobile company pamphlets which, while issued in large numbers, were usually read and thrown away. Four of the books were issued in limited editions and I have been fortunate enough to obtain all of them. Early in the search the more common titles were picked up quite cheaply but there has been a gradual upswing in prices over the years, as there has been in most fields of book collecting. The burgeoning interest in the early history of the automobile has also increased the demand for these titles. I have occasionally observed a great disparity in prices for the same titles – some too low, others too high. This has, of course, lent excitement to the chase.

I hope this work stimulates interest in a relatively new field. May those who follow turn up many new and interesting titles unknown to

CAREY S. BLISS

AUTOS ACROSS AMERICA

⁂ *1903* ⁂

[1] *Horatio Nelson Jackson.* From Ocean to Ocean in a Winton. *Winton Motor Carriage Co., Cleveland, Ohio* [1903]. 36 *pp.*, 36 *half-tone photographs, pictorial white wrappers. The back cover contains the imprint of Corday and Gross, Anti-Waste-Basket Printers, Cleveland.* *Pictured, page xii and/or facing p 4*

Cf. Winton ad on p 38 of Mad Doctor's Drive.

Jackson, a doctor from Burlington, Vermont, purchased the Winton, a two-seater, 20 horsepower touring car, and hired Sewall K. Crocker as chauffeur. The trip was undertaken to disprove the assertion that it would be practically impossible to drive an automobile all the way across the continent. The pictures and the text emphasize the hardships of transcontinental travel at that time.

Both men drove during the trip. They left San Francisco May 23, 1903, and travelled roughly 6,000 miles, arriving in New York City on July 26, 1903. They were 63 days en route, with 45 days of travel time, averaging 125 miles per day. Their route was from San Francisco to Sacramento, Marysville, California; Lake View, Oregon; Caldwell, Idaho; Granger, Laramie, Wyoming; North Platte, Omaha, Nebraska; Chicago; Cleveland; New York.

This trip has been recorded in *Motor World*, July 23, 1903; in *Contrary Country*, New York, 1905 as "Six Thousand Miles in an Automobile Car"; and in *The American Weekly*, May 17, 1953, pp. 11–12, entitled "I Made the First Cross-Country Auto Trip." A revised version with some new illustrations appeared in *The Mad Doctor's Drive, Being an Account of the* 1st *Auto Trip Across the U.S.A.* as told by Ralph Nading Hill, Brattleboro, Vermont, 1964.

I located this item, being aware of the trip, in Howard S. Mott's Catalogue 166, item 34, October 1957. A telegram revealed that the pamphlet had already been sold. Subsequent correspondence showed that it had been purchased by Thomas W. Streeter of Morristown, New Jersey. It was finally acquired by me from Streeter sale 7, item 3998, October 1969. A second copy was located in the possession of Mrs. Bertha Jackson Kolk of Burlington, Vermont. *Cf. ACKNOWLEDGEMENTS page in Mad Doctor's Drive.*

[2] *Marcus C. Krarup.* "*From Coast to Coast in an Automobile.*" *This account appears in* World's Work, *Vol. 8, No. 1, New York, May,* 1904, *pp.* 4740–54. 26 *halftone photographs in the text.*

Marcus Krarup, with E.T. Fetch as chauffeur, left San Francisco June 20, 1903 and arrived in New York, August 21, 1903. The account states that the car was a 12 horsepower, two-seater, make not given but probably a Packard. They took the central route from San Francisco to Reno, Denver, Omaha, Chicago, Cleveland, Buffalo, Rochester and Albany to New York City.

The concise account is illustrated with very good photographs. The author warns those to follow that when crossing the Sierras one must watch for (horsedrawn) passenger stages and freight wagons.

OLDSMOBILE

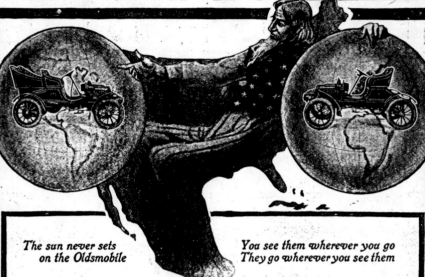

*The sun never sets
on the Oldsmobile*

*You see them wherever you go
They go wherever you see them*

All nations pay willing tribute to the Oldsmobile. Its unequalled motor equipment; the ease with which the motor is started from the seat; the device by which the spark is retarded in starting to a point where "back fire" is impossible, all emphasize its superiority, placing it in a class by itself.

Our Light Tonneau Car and Touring Runabout have attracted widespread attention by reason of their beauty of external design and perfection of mechanical construction.

Full information about the Oldsmobile line can be obtained from our nearest sales agent, or by writing direct. An interesting and beautifully illustrated automobile story, "Golden Gate to Hell Gate," will be sent on receipt of a two cent stamp. Address Dept. P.

Oldsmobile Standard Runabout, $650.00
Oldsmobile Touring Runabout, $750.00
Oldsmobile Light Delivery
   Wagon, $850.00
Oldsmobile Light
Tonneau Car,
   $950.00

Olds Motor Works

Detroit, U. S. A.

*Member
of the Association
of Licensed Automobile
Manufacturers*

Joseph N. Kane in his *Famous First Facts*, N.Y. 1934, calls this trip the first transcontinental auto trip, misspelling Krarup (Kraarup) and Fetch (Fitch). He calls the Jackson trip the first by a non-professional driver.

❧ *1905* ❧

[3] *Oldsmobile Company*. From Hell Gate to Portland. *The story of the race across the American Continent in "Oldsmobile" Runabouts, told by the men who rode and the man who looked on. Profusely illustrated by photographs taken en route. [Portland, 1931.] 46 pp., pictorial wrappers.*

With Dwight B. Huss and Percy F. Megargel as drivers, two Oldsmobile Runabouts left New York City on May 8, 1905 to race each other across the country to Portland, Oregon. The route went from New York to Chicago, Omaha, Cheyenne, Laramie, Pocatello, Boise, Oregon City, and Portland. Huss was the winner, arriving in Portland on June 20, 1905. The second car arrived on June 25 after encountering more misfortunes and breakdowns than the one driven by Huss.

The photographs of the trip occur at the top of every page of the text. Smaller photographs and some sketches are printed on the lower left and right hand corners of a number of the pages. Accounts of both drivers included.

A note inside the front cover states that "the following pages are exactly reprinted from the original booklet first published in 1905." I have not been able to locate a copy of the original.

[4] *A. C. Wheelock. "A Government Road from Coast to Coast." In* The San Francisco Newsletter, *San Francisco, Christmas Number,* 1905, *pp.* 68–69. 4 *small half-tone photographs in one montage.*

This is an account of Percy F. Megargel's second trip across the continent, this time from New York on August 19, 1905, driving a Reo "Mountaineer." As a member of the Buffalo Automobile Club, he was chosen to find the best transcontinental route. In this brief account, the route is not specified, but he arrived in Portland, Oregon, drove south to Los Angeles and in December, 1905 was on his way east. The article concludes with the statement that he would write a book on his return.

This volume appeared three years later, written by Percy F. Megargel and Grace F. Mason, entitled *The Car and the Lady*, New York, 1908. It is a fictionalized account of a transcontinental automobile race and includes incidents from both of Megargel's transcontinental journeys.

⊰ 1905–6 ⊱

[5] *Percy F. Megargel.* Three Times Across the Continent on Weed Tire Chain Tire Grips. *Weed Chain Tire Grip Co., 28 Moore Street, New York* [1906]. 8 *unnumbered leaves,* 8 *half-tone photographs concerning Megargel's trips in the text, pictorial wrappers.*

The first eight pages contain a condensed account of Megargel's two earlier trips (see two preceeding entries)

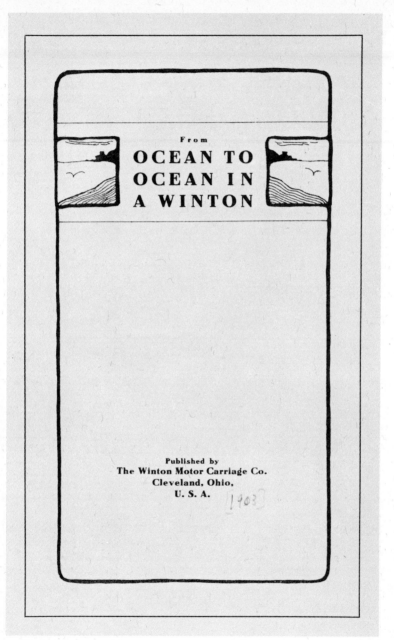

From
OCEAN TO OCEAN IN A WINTON

Published by
The Winton Motor Carriage Co.
Cleveland, Ohio,
U. S. A.

See item 1, *page* 1

THREE TIMES ACROSS THE CONTINENT ON WEED CHAIN TIRE GRIPS

BY PERCY F. MEGARGEL

WEED CHAIN TIRE GRIP CO.
28 MOORE STREET, NEW YORK

See item 5, *page* 4

and adds a few statements regarding the completion of the trip recorded in the Wheelock article. The pamphlet was written as an advertising brochure for Weed Tire Chains and the text is slanted, naturally, toward the use of Weed chains in snow and mud.

❦ 1906 ❧

[6] *L. L. Whitman. Across America in a Franklin, 1907. [New York, 1907.] Copyright, 1906, The H. H. Franklin Co. Title page, 30 unnumbered pages; illustrated with small half-tone photographs on each page and a continuing map at top of each page showing the route and the state of the roads; pictorial paper wrappers.*

Whitman left San Francisco August 2, 1906 in a six-cylinder Franklin. He arrived in New York City on August 17, time 15 days, 2 hours, and 12 minutes. He travelled the central route from San Francisco, Sacramento, Reno, Elko, Ogden, Laramie, and Grand Island, Omaha, Cedar Rapids, Chicago, Cleveland, Albany, New York City. He covered 4,100 miles using 263 gallons of gasoline, 1½ gallons of kerosene, 21 gallons of cylinder oil, 3 gallons of gear and transmission oil. He had four punctures and changed tires in Chicago. In Wyoming, he travelled 17 miles on kerosene because his gasoline ran out.

The purpose of this trip was to establish a new transcontinental record, which it did for the time being. A frank advertisement for the Franklin car, but filled with interesting comments and statistics on travel and car

5

care. Quote,"Only eight automobiles ever crossed the American continent on their own wheels."

✷ *1908* ✷

[7] *Antonio Scarfoglio.* Round the World in a Motor-Car. *Translated by J. Parker Heyes. London, Grant Richards; New York, Mitchell Kennerley, 1909. 368 pp., 70 half-tone photographs, blue cloth.*

This is an account of the Italian entry in a round the world automobile race starting February 12, 1908 in New York, westward across America, by sea to Russia, across Russia to Berlin, and ending at Paris. There were six entries: three French, one German, one American, and one Italian. The race was won by the Americans in a Thomas Flyer in elapsed time. The race ended July 30 when the Americans reached Paris four days after the Germans.

The trip across America begins on page 25 and ends on page 157. It contains 45 half-tone photographs of the trip. The journey covered the route from New York, Omaha, Laramie, south to Death Valley, Los Angeles, and San Francisco, arriving there April 10, then by boat to Seattle and by Japanese boat to Russia.

[8] *Florence M. Trinkle.* Coast to Coast in a Brush Runabout 1908. *Los Angeles, Floyd Clymer Publications, c. 1952. In print, 1971. 75 pp., numerous half-tone photographs and line drawings in the text + 2 full-page maps, pictorial paper wrappers.*

6

The author's husband picked up a Brush Runabout at the factory in Detroit and drove it in August, 1908 south to Cincinnati and west to Kansas City, Dodge City, Colorado Springs, up to Pike's Peak and home to Denver. Frank Briscoe, the manufacturer, then asked Trinkle to drive the Brush to the Pacific Coast, back to Detroit and, finally, to New York City for a winter auto show.

Fred B. Trinkle, with his wife as observer, left Denver September 28, 1908. They drove through Laramie, Ogden, Ely, Tonopah, Big Pine, south over Walker Pass to Kernville, north to Fresno, San Jose, and San Francisco. The car was then shipped back to Detroit by train. On December 20, 1908 Fred Trinkle and Harvey Lincoln left Detroit to complete the trip east. They drove through Toledo, Cleveland, Buffalo, Albany, arriving in New York City on December 30. The car was put in the auto show in New York where it attracted much attention. Fred Trinkle later received word from the American Automobile Association that he had made the 17th transcontinental auto trip. The account of the trip ends on p. 45, pp. 46–57 are advertisements and testimonials for the Brush Runabout reprinted from contemporary pamphlets.

A very well written, straightforward account of the trip, especially of the hardships from Denver to San Francisco. Good descriptions of the people and country, mentions workers constructing the Los Angeles Aqueduct.

[9] *Hugo Alois Taussig.* Retracing the Pioneers from West to East in an Automobile. *Privately printed, San Francisco,* 1910. 115 *numbered and signed copies printed on Alexandria Vellum by the Philopolis Press.* 105 *pp.,* 36 *half-tone photographs in the text, folding map, white boards.*

Taussig left San Francisco June 1, 1909, arrived New York City July 12, 1909; total mileage, 4088.5 miles. He travelled the north central route San Francisco to Los Angeles and back north via Mojave, Independence and Tonopah, through Salt Lake City, Laramie, Grand Island, Chicago and points east. Eleven page itinerary with mileage at the end. A short but succinct account with good photographs.

Quote from the preface, "The truth is, that crossing the American continent affords one but little variety of incidence. As for the people we met, I can truthfully say that we met no Indians on our way across the continent, and that the country harbored no such people as our interesting California '49er, the ubiquity of the railroad having made the entire people as one and the numberless hotels mitigating against meeting with the old time hospitality of the farmer."

[10] *Alice Huyler Ramsey.* Veil, Duster and Tire Iron. *Covina, California,* 1961. 500 *copies printed by Grant Dahlstrom at the Castle Press, Pasadena.* 104 *pp.,* 47 *half-tone photographs in the text, pictorial brown cloth.*

This was the first transcontinental automobile trip driven by a woman. Accompanied by three other women, Mrs. Ramsey left New York City June 9, 1909 in a 1909 Maxwell touring car provided by the Maxwell-Briscoe Company. They travelled the north central route from New York, Buffalo, Chicago, Grand Island, Laramie, Salt Lake City, Reno, Lake Tahoe, Oakland, San Francisco, arrived some time after August 9, 1909.

A good descriptive text with probably the best photographs of an early overland automobile trip. They used the Automobile Blue Books for guides east of the Mississippi but west of that river they had no good guides. "Many a time we found our correct route by following poles which carried the greater number of wires." (P. 77.)

Mrs. Ramsey's trip has been recognized several times in newspaper and magazine accounts. On October 20, 1960 she was designated the "Woman Motorist of the Century" by the American Automobile Association. I had the pleasure of meeting Mrs. Ramsey and assisting her in finding a printer for her reminiscences. Mrs. Ramsey has been driving across the country many times since that initial trip in 1909, including up to the date of the printing of this book.

[11] [*Overland Automobile Company*]. 5000 Miles Overland. Wonderful Performance of a Wonderful Car. The Story of Miss Scott's Journey Overland. [*Toledo*, 1910.] 51 *pp.*, 2 *half-tone photographs of the trip on every page of text, pictorial wrappers.*

This is a promotional pamphlet for the Overland Automobile of a trip taken by Blanche Stuart Scott and Gertrude Lyman Phillips, starting May 16, 1910. Miss Scott drove the entire distance unassisted covering 5393 miles in a 24-horsepower Overland. Their route was from New York via Utica, Indianapolis, Toledo, Chicago, Clinton, Council Bluffs, Kearney, Cheyenne, Denver, Laramie, Ogden, Tonopah, Gardnerville, Lake Tahoe, Sacramento, Stockton, San Francisco, arriving July 23.

A well written account with special emphasis on the western part of the trip. Although apparently guided by others with a pilot car, Miss Scott was the second woman to drive an automobile across the country.

[12] *Harriet White Fisher.* A Woman's World Tour in a Motor. *Philadelphia and London, J. B. Lippincott & Co.,* 1911. 361 *pp.,* 70 *half-tone photographs, blue cloth.*

The trip across the United States covers pp. 311–59. They arrived in San Francisco from Honolulu June 17, 1910. They left San Francisco with a chauffeur on June 26, driving a 40-horsepower Locomobile. They took the central route via Sacramento, Tonopah, Salt Lake City,

Laramie, Cheyenne, Grand Island, Omaha, Chicago, Rochester, New York City, arriving in Trenton, New Jersey, August 17, 1910.

Quote, "We had no directions except what the guide-book told us, which was to follow the old Union Pacific Railroad." The book has interesting comments about people, customs and events. Nine of the photographs relate to the trip across the United States.

✤ *1911* ✤

[13] *R. S. Monihan.* "*Ocean to Ocean by Automobile.*" *In* American Heritage, *New York, April,* 1962, *Vol.* 13, *No.* 3, *pp.* 54–65.

A photographic essay with a one-page introduction by Bruce Catton. This trip was organized by John Guy Monihan and consisted of forty people in eleven Premier Automobiles and one truck. They left Atlantic City on June 26, 1911 and arrived in Los Angeles August 10, travelling 4731 miles. The trip covered the usual middle route. In the preface, Catton mentions his own trip across the country driving with his uncle from Minneapolis to Los Angeles in 1915.

An ad on the back page of *Motoring Magazine*, San Francisco, June 15, 1912 offers a portfolio of 108 illustrations published by Premier Motor Manufacturing Co. showing photos of the trip. No copy has been located. ← *Got it!*

Mr. Monihan reports that there was no contemporary written account of his father's journey. A printed account of the trip is now being considered for publication. This information was given to me by him in a letter of May 23, 1962.

[14] *Paul H. Marlay.* Story of an Automobile Trip from Lincoln, Nebraska to Los Angeles [*n. p.*, 1911]. *31 pp., 14 full-page half-tone photographs plus 5 small photographs in the text, white paper wrappers with half-tone photograph pasted on front cover.*

The trip started at Lincoln, Nebraska, August 27, 1911, in a 30-horsepower White gasoline car, arriving in Los Angeles on September 28, 1911. They followed the central route from Lincoln to Denver, Cheyenne, Salt Lake City, Reno, Truckee, Sacramento, San Francisco and south to Los Angeles. Statistics: 2723.8 miles travelled in 1067 hours, 25 minutes, running time, using 184 gallons of gasoline, 7½ gallons of oil, 16.3 miles per hour average speed, 14.8 miles per gallon.

Although not a complete transcontinental trip, this account covers the difficult western area when such trips were few and worthy of notice. A somewhat pedestrian account with good photographs.

*unillustrated
reprint, 1984*

[15] *Victor Eubank.* "Log of an Auto Prairie Schooner. *Motor Pioneers on the 'Trail to Sunset.'*" *In* Sunset Magazine, *San Francisco, February, 1912. Pp. 188–95, 6 half-tone photographs by H. D. Ashton and one map.*

Eighteen tourists embarked in five cars with six professional drivers in the fall of 1911. The tourists paid $875

5000 MILES

Overland

Wonderful
Performance
of a
Wonderful
Car

The Story
of
MISS SCOTT'S
Journey
Overland

See item 11, page 10

FROM NEW YORK
TO LOS ANGELES
A Transcontinental Motor Trip

By SYDNEY RUSSELL

"For my part, I travel not to go anywhere, but to go.
I travel for travel's sake.   The great affair is to move."
—Robert Louis Stevenson.

See item 17, page 14

apiece for the trip. All arrangements were made by the Raymond-Whitcomb Tours with the cooperation of the American Automobile Association. They drove 40-horsepower Garford automobiles over the central-southern route, New York, Syracuse, Chicago, Omaha, Kansas City, and west to Dodge City, Trinidad, Santa Fe, Phoenix, El Centro, San Diego and north to Los Angeles.

Interesting quotation:"We were motorists as far west as Chicago. Then we became pioneers." (p. 191.) Out of this trip may have come the novel, *On the Trail to Sunset*, New York, 1912, by Thomas W. and Agnes A. Wilby. It is a fictionalized account of a transcontinental auto trip covering the same route as this tour.

⁂ 1912 ⁂

[16] *Motor Car Manufacturing Co., Indianapolis.* Photo Story of a Pathfinder, Being a Pictorial Review of the Triple Transcontinental Trek in a Pathfinder 40, 1912. [*Chicago*, 1912.] 32 *pp., blue paper wrappers.*

The preface, "Going Somewhere," by Wilbur D. Nesbitt, pp. 3–5, tells of the joys of motoring. Pp. 6–28 contain half-tone photographs of the three trips with captions. The photographs were taken by A. L. Westgard. Pp. 29–30 contain a note by the Motor Car Manufacturing Co.; p. 31 contains a testimonial by Westgard and a toast to him. Also on p. 6 is a small map of the three trips.

The three trips were all driven by A. L. Westgard. The first left New York City, June 11, 1912 on a route called the Northwest Trail, arriving in Seattle, date not given, and drove south to San Francisco. The Overland Trail trip started from San Francisco August 21, 1912 and finished at Philadelphia, date not given. The Midland Trail started from Philadelphia in the fall of 1912 and travelled the southernmost route to Los Angeles, arriving there November 25, 1912. The total mileage of the three trips was 12,678 miles.

Although the pamphlet was prepared as an advertising brochure for the Pathfinder car, the photographs are an excellent historical record of the perils and pleasures of overland motoring.

❦ 1913 ❧

[17] *Sydney Russell.* From New York to Los Angeles; a Transcontinental Motor Trip. *A two-line quotation from Robert Louis Stevenson [n. p., 1914]. 32 pp., numerous half-tone photographs in the text, green cloth.*

Carl Ruprecht and Sydney Russell left Edgecliff, New Jersey on August 16, 1913 with three other passengers. They drove a Packard Six and arrived in Los Angeles on December 30, 1913. Thirty-three days actual running time, 4,000-odd miles. They drove the midland route through Philadelphia, Chicago, Omaha and south to Dodge City, Colorado Springs, Phoenix, Yuma, San Diego, Los Angeles.

Several nights were spent in Harvey Houses which were considered very good. It is a simple, straightforward account without much detail or new information.

[18] *Packard Motor Car Company.* Twice Across the Great Silence (*cover title*). [*Detroit*, c.1913.] 13 *unnumbered pp., numerous small half-tone photographs on each page, pictorial brown paper wrappers.*

S. D. Waldon, J. M. Murdock, and J. C. Hinchman were the permanent crew and were accompanied by various passengers at different times. They left Detroit, Michigan August 28, 1913 driving a new Packard. The western trip went south through Illinois, Iowa, Nebraska, and Colorado, west through Wyoming and Nevada, over the Donner Pass to San Francisco (no date given). After three days in San Francisco they travelled south to Los Angeles. The return trip took them up the Owens Valley to Tonopah, Ely and Salt Lake City over very bad roads. East again from Salt Lake City to Denver, Columbus, Nebraska and Detroit. 7,000 miles in 48 days.

A promotional pamphlet for the Packard car, but with interesting text and good photographs.

🐝 *1914* 🐝

[19] *Effie Price Gladding.* (*Mrs. Thomas S.*) Across the Continent by the Lincoln Highway. *New York, Brentano's,* 1915. 262 *pp.,* 31 *half-tone photographs,* 1 *folding map, grey cloth.*

The party left San Francisco on April 21, 1914, travelling east via the usual central route to Reno, Salt Lake City, Cheyenne, Denver, Omaha, Chicago, Pittsburgh, Philadelphia and New York. "We drove a Studebaker car as far as Denver and a Franklin car from Denver to New York." (P. 262.) Total mileage 8,600 miles. They travelled the entire length of the Lincoln Highway, but obviously many side trips were taken.

This is the first full-size hard bound contemporary work to discuss transcontinental travel. It is also the first to mention the Lincoln Highway. The full-page half-tone photographs are definitely tourist in content but interesting because of the date. The book is sadly lacking in specific information but important for its comments on the Lincoln Highway.

[20] *Louis D. Round. "Transcontinental Log."* In The Motorist, *Official Publication of the Ohio State Automobile Association, Cleveland,* 1914. *Letters to* The Motorist *appearing in the issues of July,* 1914, *p.* 16; *August,* 1914, *p.* 19 *and September,* 1914, *p.* 12.
   This account was rewritten and expanded in
Thornton E. Round. The Good of It All. *Cleveland, Ohio, Lakeside Printing Company,* c. 1957. 10 *l.* +243 *pp., numerous full-page half-tone photos, grey cloth.*

Louis D. Round, his wife, two sons, and two daughters left Cleveland June 21, 1914 in two cars—a Winton Six and a Ford roadster—arriving at Long Beach, California on July 10, 1914. They travelled the usual route through Chicago, Omaha, Denver, then to Salt Lake City, Tonopah and Goldfield, Nevada; Big Pine, and the Mojave desert to Los Angeles and Long Beach. The return trip took them to San Francisco via highway 99, to Sacra-

Across the Continent
by the
Lincoln Highway

CAL. NEV. UTAH WYO. NEB. IOWA. ILL. IND. OHIO PA. N.J. N.Y.

Effie Price Gladding

See item 19, page 15

IT
MIGHT HAVE BEEN
WORSE

A MOTOR TRIP FROM COAST
TO COAST

BY

BEATRICE LARNED MASSEY

SAN FRANCISCO
HARR WAGNER PUBLISHING CO.
MCMXX

See item 34, *page* 27

mento, Donner Pass, Ogden, Laramie, Omaha, Chicago, and Cleveland. The entire trip covered 7,245 miles. The Winton used 811½ gallons of gasoline costing $166.70 while the Ford consumed 358½ gallons costing $59.39.

The original letters are very short with little detail except statistics. The expanded account by the son, Thornton E. Round, has some fine details of the trip interspersed with some unrelated material. Several good photographs of incidents on the trip are somewhat spoiled by being poorly printed.

[21] Chase A. Reilly. "A Pharmacist at Play." In Ford Times, Vol. 10, No. 3, October, 1916. Detroit, 1916, pp. 111–15. 4 line cut illustrations in the text.

The party started from St. Louis, Missouri, apparently in the summer of 1914, driving a new Ford touring car. They travelled the National Old Trails Route to Los Angeles arriving there after 26 days running time. Their speedometer read 4,376 miles at Los Angeles, using 196 gallons of gasoline at an average of 16½c per gallon. This route, starting in St. Louis, reached Los Angeles via Kansas City, Wichita, Dodge City, Pueblo, Colorado Springs, Santa Fe, Flagstaff, Williams, San Bernardino, and Pasadena. On the way, they made several side trips to Pike's Peak, Cheyenne Canyon, and the Grand Canyon.

A simple, straightforward account with no special reference to the Ford car.

[22] *Samuel N. Whitaker*. Across the Continent in a Ford. *Being letters to his friends, written from Phoenix, Arizona, Los Angeles, California and Moline, Illinois. Done into print by his former pals in the Dean-Hicks Plant, Grand Rapids, Mich. June* 1915. 126 *pp.*, *one half-tone photograph on the front cover, paper wrappers.*

Mr. Whitaker and his wife left Grand Rapids, Michigan, November 8, 1914 in a Ford touring car. They picked up the Lincoln Highway at South Bend, Indiana and drove west through Chicago, Moline, Illinois, Kansas City, Dodge City, Trinidad, Raton, Santa Fe, Ash Fork, Phoenix, Flagstaff, Blythe, San Bernardino and Los Angeles arriving there January 3, 1915. Left Los Angeles on return trip March 31, 1915, drove via Needles, Williams, Grand Canyon, Flagstaff, Amarillo, where they shipped by rail freight from Amarillo to Channing, Texas, because the Canadian river was flooded. Across the Texas Panhandle they drove to Moline, Illinois where the trip account closes.

This is a very detailed account of the trip coming and going. It is probably one of the best accounts of hardships and experiences of auto travel over the western roads. Pages 40–41 mention the work of the Automobile Club of Southern California in putting up road signs from Albuquerque west. Statistics of time, mileage, and gasoline expenses are given for both east and west trips.

Wellington E. Miller copy, Garden Grove, California.

[23] *Emily (Price) Post.* By Motor to the Golden Gate. *New York and London, D. Appleton and Company, 1916. xii, 1 l., 281 pp., + list of maps on verso of which is map containing complete route of trip, + 14 leaves containing reproduction of 27 hand-drawn maps, 32 full-page half-tone photographs, dark blue cloth with map of route on cover duplicated on end-papers.*

The party left New York in April, 1915. According to Mrs. Post's account, the trip took 27 days to reach San Francisco. They travelled the north central route to Cheyenne, then directly south to Las Vegas, New Mexico, west to Williams, Arizona where the car broke down. The crippled car and party travelled to Los Angeles by rail after which they drove north to San Francisco.

The text is in dialogue form, socially but not historically important. Chapter 1 points out the problems of obtaining guides and maps west of the Mississippi. The illustrations are more scenic than historic. Two chapters at the end describe what to take and wear with a daily expense account. The 28 hand-drawn maps give interesting comments on sights and road hazards.

Emily Post was, of course, the authority on etiquette who died in 1960. *Desert Magazine* for March, 1960 reviewed this trip and reproduced two photographs from the book.

[24] *J. Smith Walsh.* Ford to Frisco [*n.p.*, c. 1915]. 42 *pp., illustrated.*

Apparently the trip started from Metropolis, Illinois in April, 1915, ending at San Francisco May 26, 1915.
Title and information from L. B. Romaine Catalogue No. 125, item 156, 1953. No copy located or seen by me.

[25] *W. F. Sturm.* Picture of a Car. *Indianapolis, Indiana, Stutz Motor Car Company* [1915]. *Reprint by Floyd Clymer, Los Angeles.* [*n. d.*] *In print, 1971. 16 unnumbered pp., numerous half-tone photographs in the text.*

E. G. Baker, driver, and W. F. Sturm, observer, left San Diego on May 6, 1915 in a Stutz Bearcat, drove the southern route to Dodge City and northeast to Indianapolis and New York, arriving on May 18, 1915. The purpose of the trip was to make a record-breaking one man drive from San Diego to New York. At the end is a 4 page list of statistics of the trip.
A short and succinct account of the journey with good photographs of the car *en route* on good and bad roads.

[26] *George H. Stevens & James G. Larmer.* Transcontinental Trip in a Ford, *from Lead, Black Hills, S. Dakota to Detroit, Mich. May 25, 1915–Aug. 3, 1915.* [*Detroit, Joseph Mack Printing House*] c. 1915. 76 *pp., half-tone photographs and brief maps of each day's run in the text, pictorial paper wrappers.*

The two authors left Lead, South Dakota on May 25, 1915 driving a new Ford touring car. They headed west across Montana through Idaho to Spokane, Seattle, Tacoma, Portland, and south to San Francisco, arriving there on July 14. After visiting the World's Fair, they left San Francisco on July 19 for Sacramento, across the Sierras to Carson City, Salt Lake City, Laramie, Denver, Kansas City; took the Santa Fe trail with its red, white, and blue striped markers, across muddy Illinois to Indianapolis, Dayton, Wheeling, Gettysburg, Washington, D.C., Baltimore, New York City, Boston, Brattleboro, Syracuse, Niagara Falls, Toledo, and arrived in Detroit on August 3. They were 71 days *en route*, covered 8,450 miles in 59 days running time. The last page has a statement of expenses and mileage.

Written in the form of a daily diary, it is intended as a guide book for tourists. Judging from the complimentary remarks on Ford cars and Dayton Airless Tires, the work may have been partially subsidized by both companies. Its greatest value is the comments on roads and driving conditions. As the preface states, "...and whoever owns a motor car must have a longing to drive it across the continent..." Detroit Public Library copy.

[27] *Saxon Motor Company, Detroit*. Saxon Days [*cover title*]. *Detroit* [1915]. *22 pp., several small half-tone photographs & drawings in the text, pictorial wrappers.*

Pages 12–13 have an account of the Saxon car which claimed to be the first car to cross the continent over the

Lincoln Highway. An outline map and five photographs on a double page spread illustrate this trip. M. H. Croker and Fred Wilkins left New York June 4, 1915 (?) and arrived in San Francisco July 4, trip covering 3,089 miles, averaging 30 miles per gallon. P. 15 contains an account of the two Logan brothers who crossed the continent later that year from Tiffin, Ohio to Los Angeles via Columbus, Salt Lake City, Tonopah, Palmdale, Los Angeles.

Strictly written as an advertisement for the Saxon car which, for a time, challenged the Ford in popularity. The transcontinental account is subordinate to testimonials for the Saxon automobile. Included here because of its claim to be the first automobile to traverse the Lincoln Highway from beginning to end. This trip is not mentioned in *The Lincoln Highway*, Dodd, Mead and Company, New York, 1935.

[28] *Amelia Fry. "Along the Suffrage Trail. From West to East for Freedom Now!" In* American West, *Vol. 6, No. 1, January,* 1969. *Palo Alto, California,* 1969. *Pp. 16–25,* 11 *half-tone photographs in the text.*

Sara Bard Field and Frances Joliffe left San Francisco September 16, 1915 in an Overland touring car belonging to two Swedish women, Miss Kindborg, driver, and Miss Kindstedt, observer, who volunteered to drive them to Washington, D. C. to carry a suffrage petition to President Wilson. Frances Joliffe fell ill and left the party at Sacramento. They crossed the Sierras at Donner Pass, followed the route to Salt Lake City, Colorado

Springs, Denver, Kansas City, Chicago, Cleveland, Syracuse, Boston, New York, and Washington. Mrs. Field made speeches and attended receptions along the way. Finally, on December 6, 1915 she presented the petition in person to President Wilson at the White House.

A historical recounting of the trip with emphasis on the suffragette meetings across the country and only a few details of the journey. The Huntington Library has the original letters Sara Bard Field wrote to Charles Erskine Scott Wood while on the trip.

[29] *William Benjamin Gross. From San Diego, California to Washington, D. C. Being a Descriptive Account of the First Official Trip by Automobile Over Southern National Highway. [San Diego, 1916.] 57 pp., 12 full-page and 17 small half-tone photographs in the text, 1 map of route on pp. 30–31, pictorial wrappers.*

They left San Diego November 2, 1915 in a 1916 eight-cylinder Cadillac. The party consisted of six men in various official capacities as highway officials, publicists, and San Diego boosters. They took the southern route via El Centro, Yuma, Phoenix, El Paso, Almagordo, Roswell, Fort Worth, Little Rock, Nashville, Durham, Washington, D. C., arriving November 27, 1915. Travel time 26½ days, 3,590 miles, daily average 133 miles.

An interesting account with some good photographs. The trip was financed by the citizens of San Diego and Imperial Counties in a definite attempt to promote a southern highway with its attendant benefits to the San

Diego area. From Holtsville, California to Yuma, Arizona they drove the "New Plank Road." "The route to Murfreesboro (Tennessee) is over a toll road and about every fifteen minutes they halt your progress by the closing of a gate and some poor old woman cries out 'Fifteen cents, please, to help the poor people of Davidson and Rutherford Counties to pay for this magnificent highway.' If it were really a good road you would not feel so sore about these petty holdups, but in its present state the toll road to Murfreesboro is a disgrace." (P. 37.) These western boosters seemed to feel that western roads, maps, and information were better in their area than those through which they travelled as they went east. San Diego Public Library copy.

❦ *1916* ❧

[30] *Ezra Meeker.* Story of the Lost Trail to Oregon: No. 2. *Seattle* [1916]. 32 *pp.*, 35 *small numbered halftone photographs accompanying the text, paper wrappers.*

A trip which began on May 5, 1916 from Washington, D.C., and ended in Olympia Washington on September 12. This trip publicized an earlier journey by Ezra Meeker taken by ox-cart. The motive power was an 80-horsepower, 12-cylinder Pathfinder automobile with a prairie schooner top. The trip covered the Cumberland Trail and National Road to St. Louis, after which they travelled the Oregon Trail to Olympia.

The poor illustrations and scanty text add little to the bibliography of transcontinental auto travel.

24

[31] *Jeannie Lippitt Weeden.* Rhode Island to California by Motor. *September–October* 1916. *Santa Barbara, California, Pacific Coast Publishing Co.* [1917]. 46 *pp.* +1 *folding map,* 24 *full-page half-tone photos, paper wrappers. Presentation copy noted, dated May* 1917.

The trip started from Matunuck, Port Judith, Rhode Island about September 15, 1916. Twenty-three days later the author, her companion, a Miss Trimble, and driver Roy L. Clarke arrived in Santa Barbara after travelling 4,460 miles, driving a 1913 55-horsepower seven passenger Fiat. The trip covered the usual route through Buffalo, Omaha and Laramie. Bad weather at Laramie turned them south to Denver, Albuquerque, Flagstaff, Barstow, Pasadena, and Santa Barbara. The longest day's run was 220 miles, the shortest 70 miles.

The photographs are historically interesting, the text is brief and not especially descriptive. It ends with an appreciation to A. L. Westgard.

1917

[32] *Edwin Hager Carpenter, Sr.* Driving from the Mississippi River to the Pacific Coast Fifty Years Ago: *Diary of Edwin H. Carpenter, edited and annotated by his wife and son.* South Pasadena, California, 1967. 500 *copies printed by Grant Dahlstrom/The Castle Press.* 10 *pp.* +1 *p.,* 10 *half-tone photographs, paper wrappers.*

The family left Burlington, Iowa November 19, 1917 driving a 1913 Cadillac. They took the southern route

25

through Dodge City, Las Vegas, Santa Fe, Flagstaff, Barstow, San Bernardino and Los Angeles, arriving December 7. The last page gives mileage and expenses.

The text, in diary form, is brief and pungent with little detail. The illustrations are very nostalgic.

❦ *1918* ❧

[33] *Caroline B. Poole. A Modern Prairie Schooner on the Transcontinental Trail – the Story of a Motor Trip. San Francisco, Privately Printed, 1919. Colophon: Two hundred and fifty copies of this book were printed by John Henry Nash, San Francisco in the month of September, 1919. This is copy No. 135. 53 pp. + 1 folding map, illustrated with 11 full-page half-tone photographs tipped in and 1 small photograph tipped in beneath the colophon, grey boards with linen spine.*

This group left Pasadena October 6, 1918 in a 1913 Packard Six. They camped the first night on the desert near Daggett, drove the next day to Needles, Kingman, Grand Canyon, Flagstaff, Hopi villages, Winslow, Albuquerque, and Colorado Springs, arriving October 20 after travelling some 1,900 miles.

This account should not be included since it ended without crossing the continent. However, the illustrations, the observations of the country and the people, and the list of food carried make it an important record. This is, incidentally, the first such account that can be considered a piece of fine printing.

Quote from the appendix, p. 52: "In the country near

Dawson's Bk Shop Catalog # 500 (Nov. 1989) lists as
#313 a copy of this bk [128 of 250] @ $100.—
I got it!

the Datil Canyon, according to an article read in the *Los Angeles Times*, a man and his wife who were crossing the continent by motor, were attacked by a party of seven wolves and had great difficulty in beating them off. This happened shortly after our trip." I have not been able to verify this statement.

❦ 1919 ❧

[34] *Beatrice Larned Massey.* It Might Have Been Worse; a Motor Trip from Coast to Coast. *San Francisco, Harr Wagner Co.,* 1920. *Printed by Taylor & Taylor,* 146 *pp., map of trip on end papers, pictorial brick cloth.*

Mr. and Mrs. Massey, driving a new Packard Six touring car, left New York July 19, 1919 with two friends. They drove west through Pennsylvania to Cleveland and by boat across Lake Erie to Detroit; west and south to Chicago; north and west to Minneapolis, Bismarck, Yellowstone National Park, and Salt Lake City. Heading west across Utah and Nevada, they halted the trip at Montello, Nevada, because of bad roads and heat. Here they shipped the car and themselves by train to Reno where they drove west across the Sierra to Sacramento and San Francisco.

In 33 running days, they covered 4,154 miles on 338 gallons of gasoline at 21 to 41 cents per gallon, using 61 quarts of oil at 15 to 35 cents per quart. "Unless you really love to motor, take the Overland Limited" (p. 143). To Mrs. Massey, the trip was exciting but tiring.

The trip was inspired by reading Emily Post's *By Motor to the Golden Gate*, 1916. This is a somewhat snobbish, amateurishly written account by a couple who drove a very expensive car, but it does contain some good impressions of America trying to return to "normalcy" just after World War I. The description of the Montana and Yellowstone country is the first so recorded on a transcontinental automobile trip.

[35] *Anthon L. Westgard*. Tales of a Pathfinder. *Published by A. L. Westgard, 501 Fifth Avenue, New York* [*c.*1920]. 213 *pp.*+ 9 *leaves of testimonial advertisements, illustrated with many half-tone photographs in the text, map of routes on front end papers, half brown cloth.*

The author as a boy was engaged by a publishing firm which issued state, county, and city atlases all over the United States. He did the leg work for the distances by pushing a trundle wheel which gave him the mileage between points. In later life he was engaged in making many of the early automobile strip maps and did path finding for the Glidden Auto Tours. He travelled as an agent for the American Automobile Association and in 1911 made the first transcontinental crossing in a truck. This volume is a series of over 60 short sketches of his experiences as an automobile path finder and map maker all over the United States from 1903 to 1919.

Recognition of his contributions to this field is implicit in the testimonials to him in some of the early transcontinental automobile accounts. In addition to the historical value of the work, the text and illustrations offer spritely testimony to the joys and hardships of transcontinental motoring.

⁂ *1920* ⁂

[36] *Essex Motor Car Company*. Across America in an Essex. *San Francisco to New York, 4 Days–14 hrs. 43 min. [Detroit,* 1920.] *A fold-out brochure containing* 11 *half-tone photographs and one map.* Photo of car in Motor Life, Oct 1920 p. 53

This is an advertising piece describing a trip from east to west and from west to east by four Essex touring cars crossing the American continent carrying United States mail, the first time in history that transcontinental mail had been transported by automobile. The average time for the four cars was four days, twenty-one hours, and twenty-two minutes. All four cars travelled the central route from San Francisco to Cheyenne, Omaha, Columbus and New York and return.

⁂ *1921* ⁂

[37] *Thomas W. Davis*. Coast to Coast with the Elks. *Camden, New Jersey, I. F. Huntzinger Co.,* 1922. 367 *pp., numerous half-tone photographs, grey cloth.*

On May 7, 1921, a 20-horsepower truck (make not given) left Philadelphia with three members of Philadelphia Elks Lodge No. 2 as a vanguard for a group of Elks later to travel to Los Angeles by train for a national convention. The auto-truck bed was covered with a rain-proof canvas top similar to the old prairie schooners and was fitted out with all the essentials for camping, a forerunner of the present camper-trucks. Visiting Elks Clubs on the way, they travelled through Baltimore, Washington, D. C., Columbus, Springfield, Illinois, St. Louis, Topeka, La Junta, Colorado, Raton, New Mexico, Santa Fe, Flagstaff, and Los Angeles.

The photographs and text give a good account of the trip, especially of the hardships because of the underpowered truck which needed tows on many occasions. Noteworthy is the description of moving the truck under a low railroad bridge at Williams, Arizona, where it was necessary to remove the tires and dig out the ruts in the road in order to get through.

[38] *James Albert Davis*. From Coast to Coast via Auto and Tent (*cover title*). *J. W. Stowell Printing Co., Federalsburg, Maryland,* 1922. 70 *pp., green paper wrappers*.

The party left Philadelphia May 14, 1921 (car unspecified). They went via Indianapolis, Springfield, Illinois, Hannibal, Colorado Springs, Santa Fe, Albuquerque, Flagstaff, Needles, San Bernardino, and arrived in Hollywood on August 5. They then drove north to San Francisco and back to Los Angeles.

This is a very frank account of a transcontinental trip. The text, which in my copy has been partially corrected in ink, has almost the charm of an unrevised manuscript. Proof reading was almost nonexistent since the text abounds in errors too numerous to mention. Delightful and unrevised statements are made about scenes, people, and institutions in the west. On p. 60, for example, is a prophetic statement for 1921: "One hour a day is also devoted to military training in the high schools, throughout the state (California)–preparing for the Japs I suppose." Mr. Davis gives great recognition to the work of the Automobile Club of Southern California. The business and social remarks innocently presented in this account make it a most valuable primary source of information. The absolutely frank and unrehearsed statements taken in conjunction with the uncorrected typography lead me to believe that it was never issued for general distribution. I have not located another copy.

[39] *W. C. Scott*. Westward Ho! *A Story of an Auto Trip to the Pacific Country. [Cleveland, 1921.] 24 pp., half-tone photograph of author, tan paper wrappers.*

Driving a Stearns automobile, Scott left Cleveland June 21, 1921 for Los Angeles. The trip covered the northern route through Chicago, Milwaukee, Yellowstone Park, Spokane, Portland, Sacramento, Berkeley, Palo Alto, Los Angeles, Long Beach, and home via the Santa Fe Trail. The car was shipped home from St. Louis to Cleveland.

An ordinary tourist account with some interesting observations including a detailed description of the Stanford Memorial Chapel.

[40] *Vernon McGill.* Diary of a Motor Journey from Chicago to Los Angeles. *Los Angeles, Grafton Publishing Corporation* [1922]. *95 pp., numerous pen and ink sketches by the author in the text, red or blue cloth.*

McGill, his wife, and daughter left Chicago October 9, 1921 in a 1919 seven-passenger Wyllis Knight. They took the usual southern route to Los Angeles, arriving in Venice, California on October 29, 1921, travelling 21 days, 2,623 miles.

A simply written account with brief descriptions of scenes and events. There is a good, short chapter on car care.

From the foreword, "Any one who can drive a car can make the trip. It is not necessary to carry a gun. The mountain roads are not difficult nor dangerous...The road across the Mojave is fairly good, and I bid you join the ranks of the transcontinental motorist."

⚜ *1922* ⚜

[41] *Mary Crehore Bedell.* Modern Gypsies, *the Story of a Twelve Thousand Mile Motor Camping Trip Encircling the United States. New York, Brentano's* [*c.*1924]. *262 pp., 34 full-page half-tone photographs taken by the author + 1 map of the route, pictorial green cloth.*

Mr. and Mrs. Bedell left New York harbor by boat on February 1, 1922 with a Hupmobile car in the hold of the ship. They disembarked at Charleston, South Carolina and drove south to Florida. Travelling the length

HOW'S
THE ROAD?

BY

KATHRYN HULME

*"Now the joys of the road are chiefly these:
A crimson touch on the hardwood trees;
A vagrant's morning wide and blue,
In early fall when the wind walks, too;
A shadowy highway cool and brown,
Alluring up and enticing down . . . "*
BLISS CARMAN

PRIVATELY PRINTED
SAN FRANCISCO, CALIFORNIA
1928

See item 42, page 34

□ □

Across the Continent

TWICE *in*
THREE
WEEKS

with *a*
Model A Ford
in MIDWINTER

□ □

See item 50, *page* 41

of Florida and back, they then headed west to New Orleans via Biloxi and northwest to Little Rock to avoid the muddy roads of Louisiana, but mud still plagued them through Arkansas. They drove southwest across Texas to Dallas and Fort Worth, El Paso, Lordsburg, New Mexico, Globe and Phoenix, Coachella, Pasadena, Santa Monica, and south to San Diego. They proceeded north to Yosemite for a two weeks' camp in the valley, west to San Francisco, north to Oregon and Seattle, east to Spokane, Glacier National Park, Yellowstone, then took the National Parks Highway through North Dakota to Minneapolis, south to Chicago, and home to New York.

A straightforward account with some interesting remarks. They made frequent use of available road guides. Despite the title, there is little about camping or campsites. It is a tourist's diary with some social and political comments.

"Such fine sounding names as the Lincoln Highway, the Yellowstone Trail or the National Parks Highway may be misleading. Not yet can one spin across the continent on fine macadam, nor anywhere near it. Although there is much work being done toward improving the roads, the fact remains that most of the cross-country going is rather poor." (P. 261.)

[42] *Katherine Cavarly Hulme.* How's the Road? *San Francisco, privately printed,* 1928. *Colophon: This book has been designed and printed for the author by Johnck & Seeger in April,* 1928, *at San Francisco, California. This edition is limited to* 30 *copies.* 1 *l.,+* 112 *pp., orange boards.*

The author and a friend, Tuny (Eugenia Morris Frost), left New York City on June 1, 1923 in a car they called "Reggie" (make not mentioned), drove west through Toledo, Chicago, Milwaukee, La Crosse, then via the National Parks Highway to St. Paul, west to the Badlands, Black Hills, Gillette and Buffalo, Wyoming; Yellowstone Park, White Sulphur Springs, Chouteau, Montana; Glacier National Park, Cardston, Alberta, Canada; Calgary, Cranbrook, northern Idaho, Seattle, south through Oregon to San Francisco. Page 112 has a breakdown of expenses, including gas, oil, food, hotels, and car repairs.

This is probably the first printed book by the author of *The Nun's Story.* It is one of the best descriptive accounts of a transcontinental trip that I have read. As Miss Hulme says in her preface, "It is not the purpose of this volume to serve as a guide-book of transcontinental travel, nor to add to the technical lore of the newest phase of outdoor recreation. Its object is, rather, to present in faithful outlines a picture of the every-day routine of a mode of travel that is yearly taking a stronger hold upon the fancy of the vacationist who is weary of sticking to conventional ruts and who feels that life owes him a new thrill." There are excellent details of the pleasures and perils of motoring. The girls spent their nights in YWCA's in the big eastern cities and camped out in western parks. She describes the colors used for national highway markers and their encounter with a trail painter who painted markers on the Yellowstone Trail.

I have copy No. 1 with a presentation note from Miss Hulme. She informed me that it was given to someone at the Johnck & Seeger printing plant. Other copies have been located at the Huntington Library and the Library of Congress. Miss Hulme showed me her own copy of the work, bound in full vellum by the printers, but without a colophon leaf. It was signed by John J. Johnck, Harold N. Seeger, Samuel T. Farquhar, Lawton R. Kennedy, and Laurence Patterson, San Francisco, December 1929.

[43] [*Myron T. Gilmore.*] Our Motor Trip from Bangor, Maine to San Diego, California–A Composite Record [*n. p.*, 1923]. 22 *pp.*, 6 *half-tone photographs, tan paper wrappers.*

The party, headed by Myron Gilmore, left Bangor, Maine on August 9, 1923 driving a Franklin car. They left Boston on August 27 for the west coast. They went the usual route to St. Louis, Denver, Colorado Springs, Santa Fe, Albuquerque, Tucson, Phoenix, Yuma, via the plank road to El Centro, Jacumba, and San Diego, arriving there October 4, 1923.

The trip took 33 days of driving time from Boston and logged 4,389 miles. The short but succinct account has several good illustrations. It captures the true flavor of a transcontinental auto trip.

✣ 1924 ✣

[44] *Melville F. Ferguson.* Motor Camping on Western Trails. *New York & London, The Century Co. [c.1925]. xix, 300 pp., numerous full-page half-tone photographs throughout, map of transcontinental trip on front endpaper, map of trip through Hawaii on back end-paper, orange cloth.*

The author, his wife, three daughters, his own mother, and his wife's mother and father, eight people in all plus one dog, travelled in two cars with two small trailers. They left Philadelphia in June (1924), travelled west to Illinois, north to Wisconsin, west to Yellowstone and Glacier National Parks, south to Sacramento, east across Donner Pass to Lake Tahoe, south to Mono Lake, west across Tioga Pass to Yosemite Valley and San Francisco, south by the coast route to Los Angeles and San Diego, then north via the inland route to San Francisco again. Taking the cars and trailers with them, they went by boat to Hawaii for an extensive winter tour of the islands.

In the spring (1925) they returned by boat to Wilmington, California, and drove east from Los Angeles to Santa Fe, north to Colorado Springs, and the usual route east to Philadelphia. In 12 months, they covered 18,000 miles including the Hawaiian trip.

This account has good descriptions and details of camping life with some fine photographs of early auto camps.

✷ 1925 ✷

[45] *James Montgomery Flagg.* Boulevards all the Way– Maybe. *Being an Artist's Truthful Impression of the U.S.A. from New York to California and Return, by Motor. New York, George H. Doran Co.* [c.1925]. 225 *pp.,* 13 *sketches in line and half-tone by the author, grey cloth.*

The author left New York City on June 11, 1925 with "the motor Queen"–his wife–make of car not given. They went to Philadelphia, Baltimore, Kansas City, Dodge City, Trinidad, Santa Fe, Grand Canyon, Needles, San Bernardino, Los Angeles, north to San Francisco, east to Salt Lake City, Omaha, Chicago and return to New York.

He spent ten days in Los Angeles painting a portrait of William S. Hart. They had been advised to take the Victory Highway in Nevada instead of the Lincoln Highway, but were forced to turn back and then took the Lincoln Highway which, although under construction, was a better road. The book is written in a humorous vein with special emphasis on bad roads and poor accommodations. "There is no doubt that 300,000 cars make the trip yearly." (P. 14.)

37

[46] *Caroline Rittenberg.* Motor West. *New York, Harold Vinal,* 1926. *Half-title,* 6 *l.,* 120 *pp.,* 5 *half-tone photographs of paintings,* 3 *folding plates of trip statistics at the end, tan boards.*

Three women, including the author, left New York June 19, 1925, make of car not mentioned. They followed the Lincoln Highway to Philadelphia, Columbus, Springfield and St. Louis, where they picked up the husband of one of the wives for a chauffeur. They drove west to Colorado Springs, then to Taos, Santa Fe, Grand Canyon, Yuma, San Diego, Los Angeles, Santa Barbara, San Francisco, Portland, Tacoma, Seattle, Spokane, Yellowstone, Grand Island, Omaha, Chicago, and New York, arriving September 15, 1925, three days short of three months on the road.

Despite an unusual number of misspellings of place names, this is a good account of a typical tourist trip. The three folding charts detail each day's drive, mileage, and gasoline and oil consumed, plus listing the hotels they stayed in, with comments and notes on the roads and car performance.

❧ 1926 ❧

[47] *E. D. Fletcher.* An Account of Colonel Fletcher's Record-Breaking Transcontinental Trip: *San Diego, California, to Savannah, Georgia . . . San Diego, San Diego Chamber of Commerce* [1926]. 8 *unnumbered pages,* 6 *half-tone photographs, unbound.*

An advertising brochure recounting Col. Fletcher's trip from San Diego to Savannah. Driving a Cadillac sedan, Col. Fletcher, his son, and two companions made the trip east in the record breaking time of 71 hours, 15 minutes, bettering the previous record by 11 hours, 56 minutes. They left San Diego on October 20, 1926, and travelled the usual southern route to El Paso, went northeast from Kent, Texas through Dallas, Shreveport, Vicksburg, Montgomery, and Savannah, a total of 2,535 miles. On the western, return trip, which they accomplished in 75 hours, 35 minutes, they skirted the southern border of the United States through New Orleans and San Antonio to Kent and the same route home.

Pp. 4–5 contain a map of both the eastern and western routes; pp. 6–7 contain statistics on the two trips; p. 8 is an enthusiastic endorsement of a national highway via the southern route.

✥ 1927 ✥

[48] *Frederick Franklyn Van de Water.* Family Flivvers to Frisco. *New York and London, D. Appleton & Co., 1927. 247 pp. + 2 pp. of ads, 7 full-page line drawings by W. J. Enright, end-paper maps, yellow pictorial cloth.*

The author, his wife, and small son left New York in a Ford touring car apparently in the spring of 1927. They followed the usual north central route through Cleveland, Omaha, Cheyenne and north to Yellowstone Park; then to Pendleton and Eugene, Oregon, and south to San Francisco where they sold the car. The trip covered

4,500 miles in 37 days, camping most of the way, at a total expense of $247.83.

A well written account in a humorous vein with good chapters on what to wear and take on the trip. They used an *Automobile Blue Book* as a guide, but not too successfully, finally relying on road signs. They took the Yellowstone Trail in preference to the Lincoln Highway in order to avoid other tourists, but found the road to be very poor.

[49] *Dallas Lore Sharp*. The Better Country. *Boston and New York, Houghton Mifflin Co.,* 1928. *viii, 277 pp., frontispiece plate, green cloth.*

The author and his wife left Hingham, Massachusetts, in November (1927?), drove west through Williamstown, Utica, Chicago, Clinton, Omaha, Salina, then south to Dodge City, Las Vegas, New Mexico, Gallup, Williams, Barstow, San Bernardino, Los Angeles, and Santa Barbara. After wintering in Santa Barbara, they returned east via Salt Lake City, Laramie, Grand Rapids, and home.

A philosophical essay relating conversations between husband and wife concerning scenes and events on their trips across the continent. This author of many nature books died in 1929 and this may have been his last work.

[50] *Ford Motor Company.* Across the Continent Twice in Three Weeks with a Model A Ford in Midwinter. [*Detroit,* 1927.] *One sheet folded in thirds to make a foldout brochure of 6 pp., half-tone photograph of a Ford Model A on first page, map and account of the trip on the other 5 pp.*

Ray Dahlinger, a Ford engineer, left Dearborn, Michigan on December 2, 1927 accompanied by Mr. Henry Ford as far as Saline, Michigan. He then drove southwest to Dallas and followed the extreme southern route west to San Diego and north to Los Angeles, arriving on December 6. After a side trip to San Francisco and return, he headed east again via the same route to Dallas, then north and east to St. Louis, Cleveland and New York, north to Albany and west to Syracuse, Niagara Falls, and Dearborn, arriving on December 23, 1927 after travelling 8,328 miles.

A good, straightforward account written to promote the new Model A Ford. Undoubtedly the first trip of a Model A Ford across the United States.

❦ 1929 ❦

[51] *Maria Letitia Stockett.* America: First, Fast and Furious. *Baltimore, The Norman-Remington Co.,*1930. *xi, 1 l., 278 pp., 52 full-page half-tone photographs, half black cloth, colored boards.*

The author and two women friends left Boston in the spring of 1929 driving a Chrysler west to Buffalo. They took a Great Lakes steamer from Buffalo to Duluth, Minnesota, resumed driving northwest to Minot, North Dakota, along the Canadian border to Glacier National Park, Lake Louise, Spokane, south through Oregon and California to San Francisco, Santa Barbara and San Diego. On the return trip they went west to Zion Canyon, the North Rim of the Grand Canyon, Brice Canyon, and Ouray, Colorado where the trip ended.

The text of this work is interspersed with history of the areas through which they travelled and descriptive passages on scenic places visited. It has little worth as an account of contemporary society or events and the photographs are typical tourist views of no historical value.

[52] *Daniel Smith Crowningshield.* Jolly Eight, Coast to Coast and Back. *Richard G. Badger, Publisher, Boston, The Gorham Press* [*c*.1929]. 199 *pp.*, 16 *full-page half-tone photographs, red cloth.*

The author, his wife, and six young men left Greenfield, Massachusetts in May (1929?) driving two cars, a Nash and an Essex. They went south to Washington, D.C., then west through Ohio, Illinois, Missouri, Kansas, Colorado, New Mexico to California. The return trip took them north from San Diego to Oregon, Washington, and east to Yellowstone, the Dakotas, Minnesota, Wisconsin, Illinois, Niagara Falls, and home.

A folksy account of a camping trip across the United States and back. A few interesting comments about people and places but of no great historical value.

[53] *Paul Egbert Vernon.* Coast to Coast by Motor. *Soho Square, London, A. & C. Black, Ltd. Fifth Avenue, New York, William Edwin Rudge,* 1930. *xi,* 115 *pp.,* 1 *p.,* 8 *full-page half-tone plates made from photographs taken by the author and colored by hand, folding map of trip tipped in at the end, blue cloth.*

The author and a friend left New York in August (1929?), driving a Benz touring car. They went west through Pennsylvania, Illinois, Iowa, South Dakota, Yellowstone National Park, Idaho, down the Columbia River to Astoria; south to San Francisco and Los Angeles. They returned going east to Albuquerque, Kansas City, Cincinnati, and New York. They travelled 9,305 miles with expenses of $532.00 plus $30–$40 for tips.

Quoting from the preface, "It was a journey I had long wished to make, and for several years I had anxiously studied the conditions of the roads from the windows of the Transcontinental Limiteds, ..." An unimportant account of a well-to-do man who stayed mostly at hotels and commented very briefly on scenes and events.

[54] [*Fred Champion Salmon.*] From Southern California to Casco Bay by Ted Salmon. *San Bernardino, San Bernardino Publishing Co.* [*c.*1930]. 2 *pp.* + 321 *pp., frontispiece half-tone photograph of the author, his wife, and the car, half red cloth over marbled paper.*

The author and his wife left Los Angeles November 30, 1929 in an Essex coupe, destination Portland, Maine.

They travelled east over the southern route to New Orleans and north along the Atlantic coast to Portland. They returned through Chicago, south to New Mexico, and west to Los Angeles having travelled 10,435 miles in 70½ days including stop-overs.

A very ordinary account written by a California "booster." It is unusual only because the trip was taken in the winter and describes some hardships of winter travel.

❧ 1931 ☙

[55] *John Thomson Faris.* Roaming American Highways. *New York, Farrar & Rinehart, Inc., Publishers, 1931. xviii, 301 pp., 32 full-page half-tone photographs, folding map hinged inside back cover, dark red cloth.*

A 7 page introduction contains a brief history of American highways. This is a guide book written by a well-known author of a series of auto travel books. The work is divided into nine chapters, each one discussing a different highway. Six of them are transcontinental routes: from Washington to San Diego by the Lee Highway; from St. Augustine to San Diego by the Old Spanish Trail; from Baltimore to Los Angeles by the National Old Trails Highway; from New York to San Francisco by the Lincoln Highway; from New York to Los Angeles by the Pikes Peak Ocean-to-Ocean Highway; and from Portland, Maine, to Portland, Oregon by the Theodore Roosevelt International Highway.

The text is more historical and descriptive than useful as a route marker.

[56] *Irwin Warren Delp.* The Santa Fe Trail to California. *Boston [c.*1933*].* 174 *pp., red cloth.*

The author and seven boys left Ohio in June, (1933?), driving a Ford truck. They travelled across Ohio, Kansas and the Santa Fe Trail to California. The return trip was to be written up under the title, *The Sagebrushers Return*, but no copy has been located.

The text is written in the form of questions and answers on local history as they crossed the country.

[57] *Lewis Stiles Gannett.* Sweet Land. *Garden City, New York, Doubleday, Doran & Company, Inc.,* 1934. *viii,* 237 *pp., line drawings by Ruth Chrisman Gannett in the text, green cloth.* Reviewed in Ford News, Dec. 1934 p. 238

The author, his wife, and young son left Niagara Falls, New York, in June, 1933 driving a Ford V-8. Their route took them west to Chicago and the World's Fair; Hannibal, Missouri; Route 66 to California; north to San Francisco and west over the Tioga Pass to Virginia City, Yellowstone National Park, the Badlands, into Canada, and down to Connecticut. They travelled 8,631 miles in 38 days.

The text is divided into a series of essays on various aspects of transcontinental travel. It grew out of the author's column in the New York *Herald Tribune* entitled "Books and Things." It is filled with delightful anecdotes on literary and historical matters. For example, having been stopped at the California border for plant inspection, they were refused permission to transport 2 small cacti into the state. Instead, they mailed them to Rex Stout, author of the Nero Wolfe mystery stories, who later reported that they bloomed profusely. The chapter on Yosemite seems to foretell the present situation in the valley as he decries the "fire fall" and overcrowded conditions. A delightful book and still a pleasure to read today.

A second edition appeared in 1937.

[58] *Edward D. Dunn.* Double-Crossing America by Motor. *Routes and Ranches of the West. New York– London, G. P. Putnam's Sons,* 1933. 251 *pp.,* 80 *line cut illustrations and maps, pictorial end-papers, pink cloth.*

The author, his wife, and four children left from New York (date or make of car not mentioned). They travelled from New York to Kansas City, Santa Fe, Los Angeles, San Francisco, Reno, Salt Lake City, Yellowstone, Chicago, Niagara Falls, and back to New York – 35 days of travelling in all. The book is divided into sections, each one consisting of an account of that day's trip, listing mileage, expenses, occasionally suggested reading, and highlights of the day's run.

The book was written as a guide for other transcontinental tourists. The style is clear and straightforward as a guide should be. Each day's run is accompanied with an outline map.

[59] *Guy K. Austin.* Covered Wagon 10 H.P. *Being the Further Adventures of an English Family in its Travels Across America.* 2 *Manchester Square, London, Geoffrey Bles* [1936]. 287 *pp., red cloth.*

The English author, his wife, and two children left New York City, October 15, 1934 driving a Plymouth. They took U. S. 40 to Kansas City, then southwest through Colorado, New Mexico, Arizona, to California, staying in auto camps most of the time. The author spent the winter in Southern California and the last half of the book discusses Aimee Semple MacPherson, Father Coughlin, making movies, Chinatown, etc.

An outspoken account of an Englishman's view of the United States during the depths of the depression. He lists prices of food, lodging and car expenses. The whole family was very thrilled with the west, especially the cowboys, Indians, and the still visible covered wagon tracks.

[60] *Dorothy Childs Hogner.* Westward High, Low and Dry. *New York, E. P. Dutton & Company, Inc.* [c. 1938]. 310 *pp.,* 22 *full-page illustrations from drawings by Nils Hogner, end-paper maps, grey pictorial cloth.*

The author and her illustrator-husband left Connecticut about March 1, 1935 driving a 1929 Ford roadster. They drove south to New York City and south and west to Oklahoma, but the trip between Norfolk and Oklahoma was not recounted as being "of no consequence." They then went south and west from Oklahoma City through the dust bowl to Dallas, El Paso, Lordsburg, Douglas, Tombstone, Tucson, Phoenix, Yuma, and Los Angeles. They took a number of trips through the southwestern deserts during the next few months, then drove north through Mojave to Death Valley, east to Boulder Dam, Grand Canyon, Colorado, back through the dust bowl and east to Connecticut.

The main purpose of the trip was to see and report on the great American desert and the main value of the book is its sympathetic account of the southwestern desert. E. I. Edwards, *The Enduring Desert*, Los Angeles, 1969, p. 119.

[61] *Robert Edward Lee Farmer*. From Florida to the Far West. *Bartow, Florida, R. E. L. Farmer* [*c*.1936]. *132 pp., numerous half-tone photographs in the text, blue cloth.*

The author, his wife, and three companions left Bartow on July 2, 1935 driving west to Mobile, New Orleans, and the southern route to Los Angeles, then north to San Francisco, Eugene, Spokane and east to Glacier and Yellowstone National Parks, Salt Lake City, southeast through Vicksburg and home.

The text is mostly compiled from guides and advertising brochures with photos borrowed from the same sources. It has no real historical value.

AMERICA

FIRST ★ FAST & FURIOUS

BY

LETITIA STOCKETT

BALTIMORE

1930

THE NORMAN-REMINGTON CO.

See item 51, *page* 41

DOUBLE-CROSSING AMERICA
BY MOTOR

Routes and Ranches of the West

BY

EDWARD D. DUNN

*With 80 Illustrations
and Maps*

G. P. PUTNAM'S SONS
NEW YORK—LONDON

1933

See item 58, page 46

[62] *Mark Pepys, 6th Earl of Cottenham.* Mine Host, America. *Forty-eight Pall Mall, London, Collins, 1937. 473 pp., numerous full-page half-tone photographs, 1 map of the route, blue cloth.*

The author and a Chrysler Corporation executive left New York City in September, 1935 driving a Chrysler "Airflow" model car. Eight days later they arrived in Los Angeles after following the usual middle route to Kansas City, then south to Amarillo, Roswell, Albuquerque, and west through San Bernardino to Los Angeles. The account of the trip covers pp. 87–212.

An Englishman's view of America in the mid-thirties with comments on life, politics, sports, and America's problems, mentioning well-known people, places, and events. This is a well-written account with a few good photographs and many typical tourist photographs. There is a good index on pp. 463–73 and the appendix, pp. 460–62, contains notes on driving expenses.

[63] *Zephine Humphrey (Mrs. Wallace Wier Fahnestock).* Green Mountains to Sierras. *New York, E. P. Dutton & Company, Inc. [c. 1936]. 253 pp., green cloth.*

The author with her husband left Vermont driving a Chevrolet in the fall (1935?). They drove south and west through Pennsylvania, Maryland, Tennessee, Arkansas, Oklahoma, Texas, New Mexico, and Arizona to California. They stayed in Santa Barbara for two months, then after other side trips around California, headed east via the central route to Vermont.

Mrs. Fahnestock, who was the author of many nature books, here produced a sympathetic account of a trip across the United States and back, avoiding large cities as much as possible. Her artist-husband spent considerable time drawing and painting along the way. She mentions accommodations in "tourist homes" in the east and her first stay in a "tourist cabin" in Oklahoma. She also describes how they rescued several ducks on the Santa Barbara beach whose feathers were clogged with oil.

❧ 1937 ❧

[64] *Roland Wild*. Double-Crossing America. *London, Robert Hale Limited*, 1938. 283 *pp*., 16 *full-page half-tone photographs, outline maps at beginnings of chapters showing progress of the trip, end-paper maps, red cloth.*

The English author, his wife, baby girl, and governess drove across the country and back in a Buick pulling a 23-foot trailer. They left New York in April (1937?), drove to Washington and south to Georgia, northwest to Louisville, south and west to San Diego, north along the coast to San Francisco with a side trip to Yosemite, then north again to Oregon and Washington. They returned through Idaho, Salt Lake City, Yellowstone, Chicago, and Detroit to New York.

A well-written account of an Englishman's view of America during the depression. Among other sights, he describes Louisville during Derby Week; the dust bowl; a pageant in Eugene; a rodeo; the Ford factory; and tourist and trailer camp life with good comments on roads and travel.

[65] *Margaret Westbrook.* Highway Travelers. 68 *Days on Southern Highways. Illustrated by Betty Le Mohn. Los Angeles, San Francisco, New York, Suttonhouse Publishers [c.1939]. xv, 168 pp., 4 full-page half-tone montage photographs, line drawings at the beginning and end of each chapter, end-paper maps, orange cloth.*

The author, her husband, and another couple left southern California on January 6, 1938 driving a Buick sedan. They travelled the southern route through Arizona, Texas and Mississippi to Florida, and returned home through Vicksburg, Dallas, Ft. Worth, El Paso, Phoenix, and Los Angeles.

This work has to be read to be believed. It is a very folksy account of life and events on this 68-day trip, interspersed with very bad poetry by the author.

[66] *Mrs. Janette Cooper Rutledge.* How to Tour the United States in Thirty-one Days for One Hundred Dollars [*New York, Harian Publications,*1938]. 48 *pp., map, orange paper wrappers..*

Foreword, preface, and statistics of the trip are on pp. 3–10; text account pp. 11–48. The starting point was

Seattle, Washington, then straight east paralleling the Canadian border, south to Chicago, Detroit, Syracuse and Boston; south again to New York, Richmond, Montgomery, New Orleans, Houston, Albuquerque, Los Angeles, and north again to San Francisco and Seattle.

This is written in journal style, mentions high points of each day's trip. The total expense, though not including the car, was $76.00. Instructions and statistics are very interesting over 30 years later.

Second edition, 1939, third edition, 1940.

Library of Congress copy.

REJECTED TITLES &
INDEX

REJECTED TITLES

Many more trip accounts were examined and rejected than are recorded here. This list includes only those titles which might appear from their wording to be, or include, complete transcontinental crossings.

Around the World in an Automobile. New York [*c*.1907]. Juvenile fiction.

Mario Barone. *Heart and Will Power; Twenty Thousand Miles Through Three Americas.* New York, 1930. Did not make a transcontinental crossing of the United States.

Hoffman Birney. *Roads to Roam.* Philadelphia, 1930. Travelled only in the west.

George D. Brown. *From Coast to Coast.* Simsbury, Conn., 1923. From Catalina Island to Coney Island behind a horse!

Frank H. Clark. *Over Blazed Trails and Country Highways; the Story of Midsummer Journey.* Lisle, N.Y., 1919. A good account but only to Colorado Springs and back.

DeDion-Bouton Company. *De Dion Motorettes. A 1600 Mile Trip Over American Roads.* [Brooklyn, N.Y., 1901.] From Albany to Chicago in the summer of 1900.

Winifred Hawkridge Dixon. *Westward Hoboes; Ups and Downs of Frontier Motoring.* New York, 1924. Not a transcontinental trip, although this work was quoted or mentioned in some of the included titles.

E. M. F. Company. *Under Three Flags. Being the Story of the Flanders "20" Car Across Three Countries.* Detroit [1910]. Probably the first car to travel from Quebec to Mexico City.

[Arthur Jerome Eddy.] *Two Thousand Miles on an Automobile. By "Chauffeur."* Philadelphia and London, 1902. A fine early account of travel in the eastern United States and Canada.

John J. Espey. "The Model T Crosscountry." In *Westways*, Los Angeles, January, 1962, pp. 23–25. A few memories of a trip made forty years before by the author's father but not a full account.

Charles J. Finger. *Adventure under Sapphire Skies*. New York, 1931. *Footloose in the West*. New York, 1932. Neither title includes a transcontinental trip but Finger's works inspired others to drive the full route.

Jan and Cora J. Gordon. *On Wandering Wheels*. New York, 1928. A pleasant account of travelling by auto from Maine to Georgia.

Edith Wakeman Hughes. *Motoring in White*. New York, 1917. From Bismarck, North Dakota east to New England.

Paul Clyde Livingston. *Seeing America on the Cuff as Told to Frank Gill, Jr.* Hollywood [*c*.1940]. Selling products by car across the U.S. but not a true transcontinental auto trip.

Hector MacQuarrie. *Round the World in a Baby Austin*. London, 1933. Did not cross the United States.

J. J. Mann. *Round the World in a Motor Car*. New York, 1914. One short chapter on crossing Canada.

Melita L. O'Hara. *Coast to Coast in a Puddle Jumper and Other Stories*. Tessier, Sask., Canada [*c*.1930]. Partway by train and mostly across Canada.

Thomas J. H. O'Shaughnessy. *Rambles on Overland Trails*. Chicago, 1915. Touring in the southwest from Oklahoma to California.

Anne M. Peck and Enid Johnson. *Roundabout America*. New York [*c*.1933]. Travelled only partially by auto.

L. W. Peck. "Over the Lincoln Highway to the Coast." *Sunset Magazine*, April, 1915. A general guide to the highway but does not recount a specific trip.

Mary D. Post. *A Woman's Summer in a Motor Car*. New York, 1907. Over 6,000 miles in 6 months but all in the northeastern U.S.

Michael J. Richard. *Across the Continent with the Soakems*. New York, 1906. Travelled by railroad.

C. K. Shepherd. *Across America by Motor Cycle*. London, 1922. Unfair. Four wheels are part of the criteria for inclusion. This *is* a transcontinental trip made in 1919.

W. K. Vanderbilt. *Log of My Motor*. Cambridge University Press, 1912. European travel.

Mary Day Winn. *Macadam Trail; Ten Thousand Miles by Motor Coach*. New York, 1931. Not under her own power.

AN AUTHOR & SHORT TITLE INDEX
ONLY OF TRIP ACCOUNTS

An Account of Colonel Fletcher's Record-Breaking Transcontinental Trip, 38

Across America by Motor Cycle, 55

Across America in a Franklin, 1907, 5

Across America in an Essex, 29

Across the Continent by the Lincoln Highway, xv, 15

Across the Continent in a Ford, 18

Across the Continent Twice in Three Weeks, 41

Across the Continent with the Soakems, 55

Adventures Under Sapphire Skies, 55

Air Conditioned Nightmare, xx

"Along the Suffrage Trail," 22

America: First, Fast and Furious, 41

Around About America, xx

Around the World in an Automobile, 54

Austin, Guy K., 47

Barone, Mario, 54

Bedell, Mary Crehore, 32

The Better Country, xix, 40

Birney, Hoffman, 54

Boulevards All the Way— Maybe, 37

Brown, George D., 54

By Motor to the Golden Gate, xv, 19, 28

Caldwell, Erskine, xx

The Car and the Lady, 4

Carpenter, Edwin Hager, Sr., 25

Chauffeur, *see* Eddy, Arthur Jerome.

Clark, Frank H., 54

Coast to Coast by Motor, 43

Coast to Coast in a Brush Runabout 1908, 6

Coast to Coast in a Puddle Jumper, 55

Coast to Coast with the Elks, 29

Covered Wagon 10 H.P., 47

Crowningshield, Daniel Smith, 42

Davis, James Albert, 30

Davis, Mr. & Mrs. John W., xiii

Davis, Thomas W., 29

De Dion-Bouton Company, 54

De Dion Motorettes, 54

Delp, Irwin Warren, 45

Diary of a Motor Journey from Chicago to Los Angeles, 32

Dixon, Winifred Hawkridge, 54

Double-Crossing America, 50

Double Crossing America by Motor, 46

Driving from the Mississippi River, 25

Dunn, Edward D., 46
E. M. F. Company, 54
Eddy, Arthur Jerome, 54
Espey, John J., 54
Essex Motor Car Company, 29
Eubank, Victor, 12
Family Flivvers to Frisco, 39
Faris, John Thomson, 44
Farmer, Robert Edward
    Lee, 48
Ferguson, Melville F., 36
Finger, Charles J., 55
Fisher, Harriet White, 10
5000 Miles Overland, 10
Flagg, James Montgomery,
    xix, 37
Fletcher, E. D., 38
Footloose in the West, 55
Ford Motor Company, 41
Ford to Frisco, 20
Free Air, xx
From Coast to Coast, 54
"From Coast to Coast in an
    Automobile," 2
*From Coast to Coast via Auto
    and Tent*, 30
*From Florida to the Far
    West*, 48
From Hell Gate to Portland, 3
*From New York to Los
    Angeles*, 14
*From Ocean to Ocean in a
    Winton*, 1
*From San Diego, California to
    Washington, D. C.*, 23
*From Southern California to
    Casco Bay*, 43
Fry, Amelia, 22

Gannett, Lewis Stiles, xix, 45
Gilmore, Myron T., 35
Gladding, Effie Price, xv, 15
The Good of It All, 16
Gordon, Cora J., 55
Gordon, Jan, 55
"A Government Road from
    Coast to Coast," 4
Green Mountains to Sierras, 49
Gross, William Benjamin, 23
Harrison, Earle, vii
Heart and Will Power, 54
Highway Travelers, 51
Hill, Ralph Nading, 2
Hogner, Dorothy Childs, 47
How's the Road?, 34
*How to Tour the United
    States*, 51
Hughes, Edith Wakeman, 55
Hulme, Katherine Cavarly,
    xix, 34
Humphrey, Zephine, 49
It Might Have Been Worse, 27
Jackson, Horatio Nelson, 1
Johnson, Enid, 55
Jolly Eight, 42
Joy, Henry B., vii
Krarup, Marcus C., 2
Larmer, James G., 20
Lewis, Sinclair, xix
Livingston, Paul Clyde, 55
"Log of an Auto Prairie
    Schooner," 12
Log of My Motor, 55
Macadam Trail, 55
McGill, Vernon, 32
MacQuarrie, Hector, 55
The Mad Doctor's Drive, 1

Mann, J. J., 55
Marlay, Paul H., 12
Mason, Grace F., 4
Massey, Beatrice Larned, 27
Meeker, Ezra, 24
Megargel, Percy F., 4
Miller, Henry, xx
Mine Host, America, 49
The Model T Crosscountry, 54
Modern Gypsies, 32
A Modern Prairie Schooner, 26
Monihan, R. S., 11
Motor Boys Overland, vii
Motor Camping on Western Trails, 36
Motor Car Manufacturing Company, 13
Motor Maids Across the Continent, vii
Motor West, 38
Motoring in White, 55
"Ocean to Ocean by Automobile," 11
O'Hara, Melita L., 55
Oldsmobile Company, 3
On Wandering Wheels, 55
O'Shaughnessy, Thomas J. H., 55
Our Motor Trip from Bangor, Maine, 35
Over Blazed Trails and Country Highways, 54
Over the Lincoln Highway to the Coast, 55
Overland Automobile Company, 10
Packard Motor Car Company, 15

Peck, Anne M., 55
Peck, L. W., 55
Pepys, Mark, 6th Earl of Cottenham, 49
"A Pharmacist at Play," 17
Photo Story of a Pathfinder, 13
Picture of a Car, 20
Poole, Caroline B., 26
Post, Emily Price, xv, xix, 19, 28
Post, Mary D., 55
Rambles on Overland Trails, 55
Ramsey, Alice Huyler, 9
Reilly, Chase A., 17
Retracing the Pioneers, 8
Rhode Island to California by Motor, 25
Richard, Michael J., 55
Rittenberg, Caroline, 38
Roads to Roam, 54
Roaming American Highways, 44
Round, Louis D., 16
Round, Thornton E., 16
Round the World in a Baby Austin, 55
Round the World in a Motor Car, 55
Round the World in a Motor-Car, 6
Roundabout America, 55
Russell, Sydney, 14
Rutledge, Janette Cooper, 51
Salmon, Fred Champion, 43
The Santa Fe Trail to California, 45
Saroyan, William, xx
Saxon Days, 21

Saxon Motor Company, 21
Scarfoglio, Antonio, 6
Scenes on Old Trails, vii
Scott, W. C., 31
Seeing America on the Cuff, 55
Sharp, Dallas Lore, xix, 40
Shepherd, C. K., 55
Short Drive, Sweet Chariot, xx
Steinbeck, John, xx
Stevens, George H., 20
Stockett, Maria Letitia, 41
Stokes, Katherine, vii
*Story of an Automobile Trip
   from Lincoln, Nebraska*, 12
*Story of the Lost Trail to
   Oregon*, 24
Sturm, W. F., 20
Sweet Land, xix, 45
Tales of a Pathfinder, 28
Taussig, Hugo Alois, 8
*Three Times Across the Con-
   tinent*, 4
"Transcontinental Log," 16
Transcontinental Trails, vii
Transcontinental Trip in a Ford,
   20
Travels with Charlie, xx
Trinkle, Florence M., 6

Twice Across the Great Silence,
   15
*Two Thousand Miles on an
   Automobile*, 54
Under Three Flags, 54
Vanderbilt, W. K., 55
Van de Water, Frederick
   Franklyn, 39
Veil, Duster and Tire Iron, 9
Vernon, Paul Egbert, 43
Walsh, J. Smith, 20
Weeden, Jeannie Lippitt, 25
Westbrook, Margaret, 51
Westgard, Anthon L., 28
Westward High, Low and Dry,
   47
Westward Ho!, 31
Westward Hoboes, 54
Wheelock, A. C., 4
Whitaker, Samuel N., 18
Whitman, L. L., 5
Wild, Roland, 50
Winn, Mary Day, 55
*A Woman's Summer in a Motor
   Car*, 55
*A Woman's World Tour in a
   Motor*, 10
Young, Clarence, vii

315 COPIES PRINTED BY
SAUL & LILLIAN MARKS AT THE
PLANTIN PRESS, LOS ANGELES
FEBRUARY 1972